HOW TO USE THIS LEADER'S GUIDE

This leader's guide to *Get Acquainted With Your Bible* is designed with the following assumptions:

—adults learn in different ways.
- by reading
- by hearing
- by working on projects
- by imaginative play
- by expressing themselves artistically
- by teaching others

—the mix of persons in your group is different from that found in any other group.

—the length of your session may vary from thirty minutes to ninety minutes.

—the place where your session is held is not exactly like the place where any other group meets.

—your teaching skills and experiences are unlike anyone else's.

We invite you then to design a unique learning menu for you and your group from the learning idea selections given for each chapter.

—Begin with the Learning Menu headings.

—Keeping your group members in mind, choose those learning idea selections that best fit them and your teaching skills. (Try an activity you have not used before. The group members may surprise you.)

—Choose one or more selections for each Learning Menu heading, depending on the length of your session.

No time allowances have been included in the learning idea selections. Every group will take differing amounts of time. You might find it helpful to prepare more learning idea selections than you think you can actually use in the session. But be careful: trying to do too much during one session can be as frustrating as running out of things to do. Be flexible and open to the needs of the group members.

Get Acquainted With Your Bible has an introduction and seven chapters. This guide is designed to include helps for leading eight sessions, with the first session based on the introduction. If your group members are already familiar with the basic information about the Bible included in the introduction, you may want to omit that session. If you are using the study book and this leader's guide as a resource for a retreat setting or a vacation Bible school study, sessions may be combined, for example, sessions one and two. Omitting one or more entire sessions or rearranging the order of the sessions is not recommended, since the sessions are designed to build on one another to complete the survey of biblical themes.

Each chapter's learning idea selections are accompanied by a "Bible Background" section. This section is designed to provide additional information on the passages explored in the "Read It for Yourself" portion of the study book chapter. The leader will want to share all or portions of this information with the group members at the appropriate time in the session.

INTRODUCTION

LEARNING MENU

Build your learning menu by selecting one or more
learning ideas for each of the Learning Menu headings
below:

1. to get
acquainted
with this study
and each other

2. to consider
the
significance of
the Bible

3. to learn
about the
Bible's
origins

4. to use the
Bible itself

5. to close
the session

LEARNING IDEA SELECTIONS

1. To get acquainted with this study and each other. (These ideas are intended for use as group members arrive and before they receive their study books.)

☐ A. PUT THE BOOKS OF THE BIBLE IN ORDER
—Prepare sixty-six index cards by writing the name of a book of the Bible on each.
—Mix up the cards so they are out of order.
—Scatter them in the center of a table.
—As members arrive, start them working together on arranging the cards in biblical order without using Bibles or other helps. Use this exercise as a time of group building more than an occasion for displaying knowledge about the Bible.

☐ B. GUESS THE PERCENTAGES
—You will need chalkboard and chalk or newsprint and markers.
—List on the chalkboard or newsprint the percentages members guess for the following questions:
  • What percentage of all American adults read the Bible daily?
  • What percentage report they read the Bible weekly, at least during congregational worship?
  • What percentage say they never read the Bible?
  • What percentage of American Protestants report they belong to a Bible study group?
  • What percentage of American Protestants are able to name at least one of the four Gospels?
—Compare their guesses with the percentages given in "Quick Facts" on page 3 of the study book.
—Ask what surprises they find in the reported percentages.

☐ C. DISCUSS WHAT GROUP MEMBERS EXPECT
—Discuss these and similar questions:
  • Why are you in this Bible study class?
  • What have been barriers to Bible study for you?
—Share the information from "WARNING: Not an Easy Read" on page 7 of the study book.

2. To consider the significance of the Bible.

☐ A. LIST AND DISCUSS NAMES FOR THE BIBLE
—Share the material from "The Bible is . . ." on page 3 of the study book.
—Ask group members to list other names for the Bible. If they need help getting started, names might include "Scripture" or "the Good Book."
—Discuss what these other names imply about the Bible.

☐ B. REPORT TO THE "MARTIAN INVESTIGATING COMMITTEE ON EARTH RELIGIONS"
—Imagine that Martians have made contact with earth. They are interested in learning more about earth humans and especially about earth religions. They have sent a special "Investigating Committee on Earth Religions" on a fact-finding tour. Your group has been given the task of telling them what the Bible is. How will you go about this task? Remember, they know nothing about the Bible.

3. To learn about the Bible's origins.

☐ A. DISCUSS "INSPIRATION"
—The word *inspiration* literally means "to breathe into." Genesis 2:7 speaks of God breathing life into the first human being.
—Discuss what it means to say that the Bible is "inspired." Christians are divided on this important question. Some persons believe God "dictated" the Bible word for word to the writers of the Bible. Others believe that the writers of the Bible were "inspired" in that they experienced God in some way and then recorded those encounters. Yet other ideas of inspiration will fall somewhere in between these two views. Be sure group members understand that there is no definitive answer to this question.

☐ B. WRITE A NEW GOSPEL
—Provide time to look at and discuss "How the Gospel of Luke Came Into the Bible" on page 5 of the study book.
—Divide the group members into two teams. Call them "Thaddeus's followers" and "Mary Magdalene's disciples." Ask them to imagine they are living in the last part of the first century. They know Christ through the disciple whose name their group bears. That disciple is old now. Death is near. Ask each group to discuss what questions they want to be sure to ask Thaddeus or Mary so they can write a gospel account of Jesus.
—After permitting time for the teams to meet, call them together. Ask each team to report. Compare and discuss their questions.

☐ C. LOOK AT BOOKS THAT DID NOT MAKE IT INTO THE BIBLE
—If possible, have available copies of Christian writings from New Testament times that did not make it into the Bible. One good source is *New Testament Apocrypha*, edited by Wilhelm Schneemacher and R. McL. Wilson (Westminster, 1963–65). Ask your pastor for help in locating a copy. Do not be disappointed if one is not readily available in your area.
—Share the material in "Why Some Books Made It Into the Bible . . . And Some Did Not" on page 4 of the study book.
—Provide time for members to browse through some of the writings that did not make it into the New Testament or to read portions aloud. Discuss any observations.

4. To use the Bible itself.

☐ A. DISCOVER BIBLE STUDY TOOLS
—Many Bibles contain resources that help with understanding the Bible. Other helps may be found in additional books.
—You will need Bibles and at least one copy each of a Bible dictionary, a concordance, a Bible atlas, and a commentary.
—Ask group members to work through "Meet Your Bible" on page 6 of the study book, using their Bibles.
—Help members find the resources mentioned if they have difficulty. Ask what other resources members find within their Bibles.
—Then introduce the group members to the Bible study tools you have provided. Brief descriptions of these resources are found in "Warning: Not an Easy Read" on page 7 of the study book.
—Discuss how these resources can assist them in their Bible study.

☐ B. COMPARE DIFFERENT VERSIONS OF THE BIBLE

—Comparing different translations of a Bible passage can help a reader understand its meaning and appreciate the difficulties translators might have had in rendering a passage into English.

—You will need at least one copy of several different Bible versions, such as the New Revised Standard Version, the *Good News Bible*, the New International Version, and the King James Version.

—Ask for volunteers to read how one or more of the following passages appear in the different versions: Genesis 1:1; Psalm 23; Matthew 5:9; Philippians 2:5-7.

—Discuss:

   • What differences in meaning do you find in the different versions?
   • Which versions do you prefer? Why?

☐ C. HOLD AN OLD-FASHIONED "SWORD DRILL"

—"Sword drills" were held in Sunday school classes to help students learn how to find different parts of the Bible quickly. If not overused, they can provide a fun learning experience.

—Prepare in advance a list of a dozen or so Bible passage references, such as "John 3:16." Be sure each group member has a Bible.

—Allow a few moments for members to study the Old Testament and New Testament charts on pages 8–9 of the study book.

—As teams, group members race to find the Bible passage reference you call out. The first team to have a member read the passage and to state what major section it is from (Pentateuch, Gospels, Letters) scores a point.

☐ D. READ IT FOR YOURSELF

—Study about the Bible is no substitute for hands-on study of the Bible.

—Provide pencils or pens and Bibles for each group member.

—Work through individually or as a group "Read It for Yourself" on page 10 of the study book.

—Share any information you have gained from your own preparation on these passages or from the "Bible Background" at the end of this chapter in this leader's guide.

—**Or**, if there is time and members seem eager, take the study of these two passages to greater depth using the resources available in their Bibles or in reference tools. (If you use this idea, you should provide commentaries on the Gospel of John and on Second Timothy, as well as Bible dictionaries and concordances.)

☐ E. EXPERIMENT WITH LETTING THE BIBLE FORM YOU

—Many persons are so used to reading material to gain information that they know no other way to read the Bible. With practice, however, they can learn to read the Bible to permit its message to form their inner selves.

—Share the information in "Let the Bible Form You" on page 11 of the study book.

—Guide the members through the steps listed at the end of the section.

—Begin by reading through the steps and asking for questions.

—Then help the members relax, perhaps by encouraging them to close their eyes and to breathe deeply for a few moments. Urge them to block out any noise.

—Follow the rest of the steps.

—It will help if you or someone else leads the members in learning the psalm response before they do this exercise.

5. To close the session.

☐ A. LEARN A PSALM RESPONSE
—Putting Scripture verses to music can help with remembering. If you did not try the experiment in "Let the Bible Form You," try learning the response based on Psalm 119 on page 11 of the study book. If you are not musically gifted, recruit someone who will teach the response.

☐ B. PRAY FOR ONE ANOTHER
—Close the session with this prayer: Gracious God, breathe your words into us as we study the Bible. Amen.

John 20:30-31

We do not know from the Gospel of John itself who wrote it. At most, John 21:24 implies that the "disciple whom Jesus loved" (John 21:20) provided the eyewitness account behind this Gospel. However, many scholars say that John, who had been Jesus' disciple, likely did write or dictate this book. If so, he probably wrote it very late in his life, possibly around the year A.D. 100. Tradition places the writing of this Gospel in Ephesus, on the west coast of Asia Minor (now known as Turkey).

For our study, however, we are more interested in why this Gospel was written. John 20:31 is clear on this point. The Gospel of John was written for the single purpose of helping readers believe that Jesus is the Messiah, the Son of God, and so come to realize that they have received eternal life. John expresses this same intent in other places such as John 3:16 and 1 John 5:13.

This Gospel is not intended as an exhaustive biography of Jesus. John states that he has left some things out. But he considers what he has written to be enough to bring persons to believe that Jesus is indeed the Messiah.

Read John 20:19-29 in order to place John 20:30-31 in context. The story of "doubting Thomas" illustrates that John wrote his Gospel to help those persons believe who, unlike Thomas, do not have the opportunity to see the risen Jesus in the flesh.

2 Timothy 3:14-17

The Second Letter to Timothy was probably either written by the apostle Paul himself or, as many scholars now think, was written in Paul's name a generation later. The purpose of the letter in either case is to instruct church leaders.

The "sacred writings" and "scripture" mentioned are what we know as the Old Testament. When Second Timothy was written, the New Testament obviously was not yet compiled. Some congregations, though, might have already collected several of Paul's letters as well as a Gospel or two. The early Christians trusted in the Scriptures of the Old Testament and in the traditions about Jesus passed along from the apostles. The reliability of Scripture is the key to its authority.

The New Revised Standard Version translates verse 16 as "All scripture is inspired by God and is useful for teaching . . . " but then gives an alternative reading: "Every scripture inspired by God is also useful for teaching. . . ." What difference might this alternative translation make in the passage's meaning?

To inspire literally means "to breathe into." In what ways might God "breathe into" Scripture? Scripture is useful for Paul because it teaches the Christian what to believe and how to act in life. Moreover, the Old Testament Scriptures testify to the coming of Christ and thus guide the Christian toward salvation.

One of the major reasons why the Second Letter of Timothy was written was to oppose persons who misled the Christian communities about what to believe and how to live. They are described in 2 Timothy 3:1-9. Paul contrasts Timothy and himself with those "wicked people and impostors" who deceive others and who are deceived (verse 13). He urges Timothy to hold on tight instead to the traditional teachings of the church, as found in what the apostles and the Jewish Scriptures say. In other words, Paul says that the apostles' teaching and the Old Testament provide boundaries for sound Christian belief and living.

CHAPTER 1

GOD
YEARNS
FOR A
PEOPLE

LEARNING MENU

Build your learning menu by selecting one or more learning ideas for each of the Learning Menu headings below:

1. to look at the biblical accounts of how God created human beings in God's image

2. to consider the story of the first sin and what sin has meant for relationships between humanity and God

3. to contemplate the depth of God's yearning for a people

4. to close the session

LEARNING IDEA SELECTIONS

1. To look at the biblical accounts of how God created human beings in God's image.

☐ A. TELL THE STORY FROM MEMORY
—Everyone needs to have a Bible.
—Even if most group members have not been a part of a Bible study group in the past, they will likely know pieces of the story of Adam and Eve. Some pieces will be accurate according to the Bible's account; some will be recalled from popular versions.
—As group members arrive, ask them to work together to prepare, without reading the biblical accounts, to tell the story of the creation of the first human beings and their temptation. Have a designated storyteller tell the group members' recollected version of the story.
—Then compare their version with a reading of the account from Genesis 1:26–3:24.
—Discuss which parts of the group members' recollected version were not like the Bible's account.

☐ B. NOTE TRUTHS TOLD IN THE TWO ACCOUNTS OF THE CREATION OF HUMAN BEINGS
—Ask volunteers to read Genesis 1:26-31 and Genesis 2:4b-9, 15-25.
—Point out the chart in "God Creates Human Beings" on page 13 of the study book.
—Discuss:
  • What important truths do both stories convey?
  • What important truths does one account convey that the other does not?
  • Do the two stories contradict each other on any important details or truths?
—Ask group members to name the most important truths they find in these two accounts.

☐ C. INVENT A HUMAN BEING
—Discuss the following question as a whole group, or divide into two or more small groups to discuss: If you were to "invent" a human being, how would you do it?
—**Or**, divide into groups of three. Assign each group a profession or occupation, such as lawyer, school teacher, farmer, and so forth. Imagining that they are members of their group's assigned profession or occupation, ask each group to design the perfect human being. Share each group's design with the whole group.

☐ D. EXPRESS GRATITUDE FOR YOUR HUMANITY
—Discuss the following question as a whole group or in small groups: For what human attribute are you the most grateful to God?
—**Or**, working as individuals or small groups, write prayers or poems expressing gratitude to God for some particular human attribute.

☐ E. EXPLORE THE IMAGE OF GOD WITHIN YOU
—Ask members to reflect on and respond to the following questions:
  • How is the image of your mother or father present in you?
  • What makes you similar to that parent?

—Then share the information found in "What Is the Image of God?" found on page 13 of the study book.

—Ask, What about yourself is in the image of God?

☐ F. FASHION A HUMAN BEING OUT OF CLAY
—You will need modeling clay, paper towels, and facilities to wash up afterward.

—Some adults express ideas and feelings better with creations of their hands than with words. After reading the account of the creation and temptation of the first human beings in Genesis 1:26–3:24, have members work with modeling clay to fashion a representation of one of the first human beings. Place no limit on what elements or portions of the story they are to represent.

—Provide time at the end of the session for persons to share what they wish to share about their clay representation.

—This learning idea selection could also follow time spent by members in working through "Read It for Yourself" on page 16 of the study book.

—This learning idea selection could take most of your session time, so be careful not to plan too much else if you choose this learning idea.

2. To consider the story of the first sin and what sin has meant for relationships between humanity and God.

☐ A. READ IT FOR YOURSELF
—Group members will need pencils or pens and Bibles, as well as their study books.

—Work through individually or as a group "Read It for Yourself" on page 16 of the study book.

—Share any information you have gained from your preparation or from the "Bible Background" at the end of this lesson in this leader's guide.

—Draw the group members' attention to the material found in "What's in a Name?" and "Humanity's Sin and God's Judgment, Mercy, and Grace" found on page 15 of the study book.

—Discuss the questions in "Read It for Yourself," page 16 of the study book. See "Bible Background" for ideas of the directions this discussion might take.

☐ B. JUGGLE GOD'S COMMISSION TO HUMANITY
—Although not a part of the story of the first temptation, Genesis 1:26-30 speaks of God's intentions for and commissions to humanity—intentions and commissions that humanity has violated.

—Read Genesis 1:26-30 and draw attention to the sketch in "God's Commission to Humanity," found on page 14 of the study book.

—Discuss:
   • If we think of the four parts of God's commission to humanity as balls to be juggled, how can human beings keep all four balls in the air at the same time?
   • Which balls has humanity dropped, and how?
   • Which balls are we guilty of dropping, and how can we pick them up again?

☐ C. TELL THE GENESIS 3 STORY FROM DIFFERENT VIEWPOINTS
—Divide the class members into three groups. Ask each group to prepare to tell the temptation story of Genesis 3 from one of these perspectives: the first man, the first woman, the serpent.

—When the small groups have reported to the whole group, discuss the different perspectives.

☐ D. CONSIDER RESPONSIBILITY FOR SIN
—Sin might be a difficult idea for many persons to understand. We tend to talk about mistakes, personality problems, misunderstandings, and personal lifestyle preferences instead of about sin. Avoiding talking about sin is one way in which we avoid responsibility for sin.
—Because *sin* is a word we avoid using regularly, you might want to begin this learning idea selection with a general discussion seeking to define sin. One way to start this discussion is to read Genesis 3 and to ask, What was the sin of the first man and the first woman?
—Several responses are possible. Among those answers are that the humans tried to take God's place, that they decided not to trust God's guidance, or that they simply disobeyed God's command.
—Allow time to complete the chart in the section "Choices" on page 17 of the study book.
—Share answers and discuss what group members consider to be the relationship between choices and responsibility.
—Share information from "The Great Cover Up" on page 18 of the study book. Discuss the questions asked at the end of that section.
—One way of starting discussion on avoiding and accepting responsibility is to bring in a week's worth of newspapers. Ask group members to note or clip articles concerning examples of persons seeking to avoid or accept responsibility for mistakes or wrongdoing.
—You may wish to provide time for group members to work through privately the material in "For Your Eyes Only" on page 17 of the study book. If there is not time during the session, encourage group members to work on that section later. Warn them it may raise some serious issues in their lives. If members have private concerns that you cannot help them with, urge them to talk with their pastor or another helping professional.
—This learning idea selection can turn into serious discussion. Be sure to plan ample time.

3. To contemplate the depth of God's yearning for a people.

☐ A. CONSIDER GOD'S MERCY IN THE MIDST OF JUDGMENT
—If you have not already done so, point out the section "Humanity's Sin and God's Judgment, Mercy, and Grace" on page 15 of the study book. This section shows how God loved the first human beings even after they sinned.
—Discuss what this information says about God's feelings toward humanity and about God's yearning for a people.

☐ B. LET THE BIBLE FORM YOU
—If you did not experiment with reading the Bible to let it form you spiritually in the introductory session, share the information found in "Let the Bible Form You" in the Introduction, page 11 of the study book.
—Then proceed to "Let the Bible Form You" in the first chapter of the study book, pages 18–19. Share the information provided there.
—Guide the group members through the steps listed at the end of that section so they may experience Psalm 8 formationally.
—It will help if you or someone else leads the members in learning the psalm response before trying this procedure.

4. To close the session.

☐ A. SING A HYMN ABOUT CREATION
—Be sure to have hymnals for group members to use.
—You might want to close this session by singing "This Is My Father's World," "Morning Has Broken," or "All Things Bright and Beautiful."

☐ B. PRAY TOGETHER
—You might close by joining together in saying the prayer printed in the margin on page 17 of the study book.

BIBLE BACKGROUND

Genesis 1:26-31

Genesis offers two versions of God's creation of human beings. This first account is found within the story of creation in which God creates all that is in six days and rests on the seventh day after pronouncing it all to be "very good" (Genesis 1:1–2:4a).

Many persons have puzzled over why God said, "Let *us* make humankind in *our* image, according to *our* likeness" (verse 26, italics added). To whom would God be speaking? Some Christian thinkers believe that God is speaking among the three persons of the Trinity. Others offer the theory that God might be speaking to the heavenly court of angels and other spiritual beings. We cannot say for sure why God speaks in the plural here.

The substance of the "image of God" created within humanity also provokes debate. One major theory is that the image of God has something to do with the commission of dominion over all living things. In other words, according to this theory, to share in the image of God means that human beings share in God's lordship over creation.

Humans are plainly a unique part of creation. God speaks directly only to human beings among all creation. Furthermore, God will be visible only through human beings. The first commandment will forbid the making of any image of God. Humanity will be God's only image.

Further information about the "image of God" may be found in the study book on page 13.

In this version of the creation story, male and female human beings are created simultaneously, both in God's image. Both are blessed in verse 28, and both are given the charge to reproduce and to fill and subdue the earth.

Nowhere does Genesis 1 state the purpose for human dominion over the earth. From verses 29-30, one may guess that God intends all humans to desire good for all creation. There is to be no killing for food; the first humans are placed on a vegetarian diet. All animals exist side by side in peace. (In Genesis 9:3, God grants Noah and his descendants meat for food.)

As created by God, everything about humanity, and all the rest of creation, is "very good." *

Genesis 2:4b–3:24

Much of the Bible background on this second version of the creation of humanity is given in the study book, page 15.

In this version God creates the first human before the rest of living creation. Verse 7 implies that the human being is both creaturely (in its formation from the dust of the earth) and spiritual (in being brought to life by God's breath). As in the first story, there can be no doubt that it is simply by an act of God's will that God creates human beings.

Verses 18-21 imply that human beings require relationships with others who are like themselves in order to be fully human. The creation of the woman from the man's rib (verses 21-23) does not necessarily mean that the woman is either subordinate or equal to the man. This part of the story does not intend to comment on woman's status in relation to man's. The point is that the man rejoices that the woman is "flesh of my flesh." Together, they are a complete creature.

The temptation story of Genesis 3 tells of the dramatic choice humanity made regarding whether to live according to God's terms or its own terms. Humanity rejected God and chose to try its own way of life. The "I" language of Genesis 3:10-13 shows how self-conscious and pre-occupied with themselves the humans became.

Genesis 3 does not so much try to explain how evil came into the world as to describe the fact that humanity chose freely to rebel against God.

And yet God's grace prevails at the end of this story. Even though in Genesis 2:17 God makes it clear that death will follow disobedience, at the end of Genesis 3, God permits the first humans to live in spite of their disobedience. They are, however, sentenced to a hard life before death finally comes.

In Genesis 3:21, God makes "garments of skins" to replace the fig-leaf loincloths the man and woman have made to cover their shame at their nakedness. Think of what it must have cost God to sacrifice some of God's animals to make those garments in order to provide some protection and comfort to the first humans out in the world beyond Eden. God's mercy and love directed toward the first humans reveals the depth of God's yearning for a people.

CHAPTER 2

GOD
CHOOSES
A
PEOPLE

LEARNING MENU

Build your learning menu by selecting one or more learning ideas for each of the Learning Menu headings below:

1. to meet Abraham and Sarah

2. to learn how God chose Abraham and Sarah to be the first of a chosen people

3. to explore the meaning of covenant

4. to consider what faith is

5. to close the session

LEARNING IDEA SELECTIONS

1. To meet Abraham and Sarah.

☐ A. CATCH UP WITH WHAT YOU MISSED

—The survey quality of *Get Acquainted With Your Bible* means that we will study only a few major stories in the Bible. However, users will find it helpful to know some additional stories. For example, knowing what happened after the first man and the first woman left Eden will help set the stage for understanding meanings contained in the stories of Abraham and Sarah.

—As group members arrive, divide them into three work teams. Assign one of these stories to each team to research and prepare to tell in their own words:

  • Cain and Abel—Genesis 4:1-16;
  • Noah and the Ark—Genesis 6:5-22 (if anyone wants to read the entire story, it continues to Genesis 9:17);
  • The Tower of Babel—Genesis 11:1-9.

—After each group tells their story, ask: What, if any, themes seem to appear in each story?

—Allow time to read "Humanity's Predicament," page 21 of the study book.

—Ask: What parallels do you see between any of these three stories and our time?

☐ B. LEARN ABOUT ABRAHAM'S AND SARAH'S TIME AND PLACE

—As group members arrive, or after the session has begun, provide time to read the sections "The Days of Abraham and Sarah" and "The Travels of Abraham and Sarah," beginning on page 22 in the study book.

—Ask group members to look at the map on page 23 of the study book. Invite them to locate Ur, Haran, Shechem, Bethel, the Negeb, and Egypt and to note the probable routes Abraham and Sarah took between those destinations.

—If time and resources permit, provide copies of Bible atlases in which group members might look for more information about the journeys of Abraham and Sarah.

—Ask: What new bits of information did you discover about the times and places of Abraham and Sarah?

  • What distances did you note between the various destinations of Abraham and Sarah?
  • How long might it have taken them to travel those distances on foot with pack animals?

☐ C. LOOK AT ABRAHAM'S AND SARAH'S PREDICAMENT

—Ask a volunteer to read Genesis 15:1-6 aloud.

—If you have not already done so, summarize the material in "Humanity's Predicament," page 21 of the study book, or allow time for group members to read the section.

—Discuss: What was Abraham's and Sarah's predicament?

  • Without God's promises and intervention, what was the best for which Abraham and Sarah could hope?
  • What modern image or metaphor might be substituted for Abraham's and Sarah's childlessness to represent hopelessness?

—If you have time, work as a whole group to retell Genesis 15:1-6 as a contemporary story using a modern metaphor for hopelessness.

—Discuss how God might enter into the contemporary story.

☐ D. HOPE FOR THE FUTURE
—If you have not already done so, allow time for group members to read "Humanity's Predicament," page 21 of the study book. Also draw attention to God's three promises listed on page 25 of the study book.
—God's three promises indicate three ways in which God would transform the future for Abraham and Sarah and provide them with a reason to hope.
—Invite group members to write their own "wish list" of three items they would wish for in order to transform their future into one of hope. Share lists and discuss in what ways God acts to transform the future and to provide hope.

☐ E. WRITE ABRAHAM'S AND SARAH'S BIOGRAPHIES
—Divide the group into two teams—one to study the life of Abraham and the other to study the life of Sarah.
—Assign the teams the task of gathering material for biographies of Abraham and Sarah from Genesis 12:1–25:18. Teams might want to divide these chapters among their members in order to digest the information rapidly. Teams are especially to look for clues about the *character* of their individual: What do they think Abraham or Sarah was *really* like as a person? They are then to write a first paragraph introducing the biography they would have written had they more time.
—Share and discuss the biography introductions.

2. To learn how God chose Abraham and Sarah to be the first of a chosen people.

☐ A. NAME YOURSELF
—Invite group members to share examples of and reasons for changing one's name. For example, the writer of this book legally changed his last name from *Kilbourne* to *Ball-Kilbourne* in order to symbolize equality in the relationship with his wife and to honor his wife's family. Other persons might informally have begun using, or answering to, a nickname.
—Summarize, or provide for group members to read, the material in "What's in a Name?" found on page 24 of the study book.
—Ask: If you could re-name yourself, what name would you take; and why?

☐ B. WRITE FOR THE TABLOIDS
—Read aloud the following Bible passages about Abraham and Sarah. After each one, pause to invite group members to brainstorm headlines that might appear on the front cover of a supermarket tabloid in connection with a sensationalized account of the passage.
  • Genesis 12:10–13:1
  • Genesis 15
  • Genesis 16:1-16
  • Genesis 18:1-16; 21:1-7

☐ C. CHOOSE TO BE CHOSEN
—God's call to and covenant with Abraham and Sarah appears in Genesis 12:1-3; Genesis 15; Genesis 17:1-22; and Genesis 18:1-19. These four passages possibly represent different ancient traditions about Abraham and Sarah.
—Ask group members to read these four passages individually or in four small groups.
—Discuss the similarities and differences among the passages.

—Ask: What criteria do you think God might have used to choose Abraham and Sarah?
  • What evidence of criteria appears in the Scripture passages?
  • Was God's choice of Abraham and Sarah done arbitrarily? in the freedom of God's sovereign will? with some criteria in mind?

3. To explore the meaning of *covenant.*

☐ A. EXPLORE WHAT *COVENANT* MEANS
—As individuals, small groups, or in the entire group, work through "Covenant: A Thread Woven Throughout the Bible," beginning on page 24 of the study book, following the instructions contained there.
—If you have not already done so, look at the stories of the covenant with Abraham and Sarah found in Genesis 15; Genesis 17:1-22; and Genesis 18:1-19.
—Additional exploration of the meaning of *covenant* might be undertaken in dictionaries, Bible dictionaries, and theological wordbooks.
—As a group, develop a list of synonyms for *covenant.* Which, if any, seem to be exact synonyms?
—Discuss: How would you define the biblical understanding of the word *covenant* for
  • a five-year-old?
  • an atheist?
  • a lawyer?
  • an extraterrestrial, intelligent being?
  • an average, North American, citizen-on-the-street?

☐ B. RESEARCH OTHER BIBLICAL COVENANTS
—If you have not already done so, summarize or have the group read the material in "Covenant: A Thread Woven Throughout the Bible," beginning on page 24 of the study book.
—Divide the group into two to six small groups, depending on the number of members you have. Assign the following Bible passages for the groups to research and report on concerning the meaning of *covenant:*
  • Deuteronomy 5:1-21   • Jeremiah 31:31-34
  • Joshua 24:1-28   • Luke 22:14-20
  • 2 Samuel 7   • 1 Corinthians 11:23-26

☐ C. THINK ABOUT CHURCH MEMBERSHIP AS A COVENANT
—Obtain copies of your congregation's ritual for uniting with the church as a new member. This service can usually be found in a hymnal, worship book, or ritual book. Ask your pastor for help.
—Ask your group to study the membership ritual and to identify ways in which it appears to be a covenant.
—Discuss: When you join the church, what is expected of you?
  • What do you expect of the church?
  • What do you expect of God?
  • Do you think something different should be in the membership ritual?

4. To consider what faith is.

☐ A. READ IT FOR YOURSELF
—Individually or as a group, work through "Read It for Yourself," pages 25–26 of the study book.

—Share any information you have gained from your preparation on these passages or from the "Bible Background" at the end of this lesson in this leader's guide.
—Discuss the questions contained in the article.

☐ B. CONSTRUCT A MODEL OF FAITH
—You will need a child's Tinkertoy (building block) set for this activity.
—In two or more groups, work on constructing a model of what faith looks like, using pieces from a Tinkertoy (building block) set.
—This activity might prove helpful for those adults who express themselves better in shapes or in artistic creations than in spoken or written words.

C. OFFER HOSPITALITY
—Read Genesis 18:1-15 aloud.
—If you have not already done so, you might want to summarize material from "Read It for Yourself," beginning on page 25 of the study book.
—As an option, you might share information on the word *hospitality* as found in a Bible dictionary or a regular dictionary.
—Focus on the hospitality Abraham and Sarah offered to the three strangers. Discuss: What do you think the motives of Abraham and Sarah were?
  • What might have happened if Abraham and Sarah had not offered hospitality?
  • What connections do you think there might be between faith and hospitality? What risks did Abraham and Sarah run and what kinds of trust did they display by offering hospitality?
  • What contemporary examples of hospitality can you describe that exhibit faith?

☐ D. LAUGH
—Discuss the different kinds of laughs group members can describe or demonstrate.
—Laughter occurs at several key places in the Abraham and Sarah stories. Read each of the following passages. Pause after each one to discuss what kind of laughter appears in the passage. Encourage class members to re-enact the kind of laughter they think occurred.
  • Genesis 17:15-17
  • Genesis 18:9-12
  • Genesis 21:1-7
—Discuss: In what ways might laughter be an act of faith?

5. To close the session.

☐ A. LET THE BIBLE FORM YOU
—Share the information provided in "Let the Bible Form You" on page 27 of the study book. Guide the group members through the steps listed at the end of that section so they may experience Psalm 146 formationally.

☐ B. PRAY TOGETHER
—You might close by joining together in praying or singing the words of the hymn "I'll Praise My Maker While I've Breath," page 27 of the study book.

BIBLE BACKGROUND

The Abraham and Sarah Stories

You will find more material about Abraham and Sarah in Genesis 11:26–25:18 than you can cover in one session. However, you might want to read the entire passage for your information and in case questions arise during the session. To guide your reading, here is a listing of the stories about Abraham and Sarah:

Genesis 11:26-32	Abram's immediate family; his father, Terah, takes him and Lot (Abram's nephew) from Ur to Haran
Genesis 12:1-9	God's call to Abram; Abram, Sarai, and Lot move to Canaan
Genesis 12:10-20	Abram and Sarai move to Egypt for famine relief; Abram passes Sarai off as his sister to the pharaoh
Genesis 13:1-18	Abram and Lot split up territory with Abram receiving land in Canaan
Genesis 14	Abram's people defeat four kings
Genesis 15	God makes a covenant with Abram and Sarai
Genesis 16	Ishmael is born to Abram and Hagar
Genesis 17	God changes Abram's and Sarai's names to Abraham and Sarah
Genesis 18:1-15	Abraham and Sarah provide hospitality to three visitors
Genesis 18:16–19:29	God destroys Sodom and Gomorrah despite Abraham's intercession
Genesis 20	Abraham passes Sarah off as his sister to King Abimelech
Genesis 21:1-21	Isaac is born, and Hagar and Ishmael are sent away
Genesis 21:22-34	Abraham and Abimelech argue over water rights
Genesis 22:1-19	God commands Abraham to sacrifice Isaac
Genesis 23	Sarah dies, and Abraham buys a burial place
Genesis 25:1-18	Abraham dies

Genesis 18:1-15

Much of the Bible background on this story is given in the study book, pages 22–23.

"The LORD appeared to Abraham . . ." Despite the fact that three men, or the Lord and two angels, are mentioned further on, we are to have no doubt that this passage recounts an encounter among God, Abraham, and Sarah.

In the early part of this passage, however, there is no indication that Abraham knew he was dealing with God. The hospitality he offers is only normal, if generous, semitic hospitality. Strangers traveling in the desert were often dependent upon the goodwill and sustenance provided by residents of a region. A meal of bread and water might mean one more day's life.

Although Abraham's offer of food and drink is modest, the preparations he urges upon Sarah are extravagant. He calls for approximately twelve quarts of flour to be made into cakes; and he slaughters a choice calf. As a good host, Abraham hovers over his guests to serve them as they eat. Yet there is no indication that Abraham knew his guests were divine. Abraham's and Sarah's generous hospitality indicate their righteousness and their faith that they have sufficient provisions to share. They were good, kind, faithful people. Centuries later, the writer of Hebrews 13:2 would advise Christians to offer the same sort of hospitality.

In verses 9-15, the Lord promises a son to Abraham and Sarah. Eavesdropping, Sarah responds with disbelieving laughter. When challenged, she lies, denying she laughed. Although this old couple would later be held up as exemplars of faith, as in Hebrews 11:8-12, the irony of this passage is that Abraham and Sarah found God's promise of a son and future descendants too much to believe. But if that fact is the irony, the miracle of this passage is that God followed through on the promise anyway.

GOD
DELIVERS
THE
PEOPLE

LEARNING MENU

Build your learning menu by selecting one or more
learning ideas for each of the Learning Menu headings
below:

1. to identify
oppression, as
seen in the
Egyptian
enslavement of the
Israelites

2. to see God's
response to
oppression

3. to consider
ways to work
with God
toward
deliverance

4. to close the
session

LEARNING IDEA SELECTIONS

1. To identify oppression, as seen in the Egyptian enslavement of the Israelites.

☐ A. START WITH BACKGROUND TO THE BOOK OF EXODUS
—As group members arrive, ask them to read "What's in a Name?" (page 31 in the study book), "How Did the Hebrews Get to Egypt?" (page 29 in the study book), and any introduction to the Book of Exodus found in their Bible.
—Share and discuss any pieces of new information or surprises.

☐ B. IDENTIFY OPPRESSION
—As individuals, small groups, or the entire group, work through "Oppression" on page 29 of the study book.
—Ask the whole group to brainstorm characteristics of oppressors and of victims as you list them on newsprint or chalkboard.
—Discuss: What was so wrong with what the Egyptians did?
—As a whole group identify and discuss modern examples of oppression.

☐ C. READ THE NEWSPAPER
—Collect newspapers and news magazines. As group members arrive, ask them to browse through the newspapers and magazines, clipping articles or photographs telling about modern examples of oppression.
—Discuss: What makes this an incident of oppression?
  • What would make this situation better?
  • How might improvement happen?
  • What are some synonyms for oppression?

☐ D. LET THE SHOE FIT
—Discuss: In what ways is oppression visible in our community?
  • In what ways has our church participated (perhaps unwittingly) in the oppression of a person or persons?

☐ E. IMAGINE BEING A VICTIM
—As group members arrive, ask them to read "Oppression" on page 29 of the study book and Exodus 1:8–2:10.
—Invite the group members to imagine themselves in the position of the Israelites as described in the Bible passage. Ask them what ways, besides those mentioned in the Bible passage, can they think of to outwit their oppressor in order to survive.

☐ F. SHARE EPISODES OF OPPRESSION
—This learning activity can be a very powerful and possibly healing one. However, it will require special sensitivity on the leader's part. It requires that a high level of trust exist within the group. And it might be time-consuming.
—As individuals or as a group, work through "Oppression" on page 29 of the study book. Then read Exodus 1:8–2:10.
—Offer the opportunity for persons to talk about occasions when they were victims of oppression.
—Ask: How does this Bible passage interpret what happened or is happening to you?

2. To see God's response to oppression.

☐ A. CONSIDER SALVATION
—Read or summarize the information found in "God Keeps God's Promises" (page 30 in the study book) and "The Cost of Salvation" (page 33 in the study book).
—Discuss: In what ways did God bring good in spite of or through evil?
  • In what ways is the Exodus—the event in which God delivered Egypt from slavery—an example of salvation?
  • How would you define salvation?
  • How does your definition of salvation relate to the Exodus?

☐ B. THINK ABOUT THE PLAGUES
—Look at the list of "The Ten Plagues" on page 33 of the study book. Group members might be asked to find and read the Bible passages indicated.
—Examine the plagues one by one: What would you have noticed during the plague with each of your senses—sight, sound, smell, taste, and touch?
   How might this plague have pressured or persuaded Pharaoh to give up the Egyptian enslavement of the Israelites?
—Discuss: Put yourself in the place of an ordinary Egyptian. At what point would you have been persuaded to let the Israelites go?
  • Do "plagues" occur today in response to oppression?

☐ C. COUNT THE COST
—Divide the group into two smaller groups.
—Ask the groups to read "The Cost of Salvation" (page 33 in the study book).
—Have the two groups debate the question: Did the end of liberating the Israelites from slavery justify the means? Assign one group to argue in favor of answering yes to the question and the other to argue in favor of answering no.
—Discuss: What parallels might be drawn between the Exodus and contemporary situations?

☐ D. VIEW THE EXODUS AS ISRAEL'S KEY HISTORICAL EVENT
—Summarize the information in "The Cost of Salvation" found on page 33 of the study book.
—Assign individuals or teams to study one or more of the following passages:
  • Exodus 12:1-28
  • Exodus 15:1-18
  • Psalm 78
  • Psalm 105
  • Psalm 106
  • Isaiah 43:4-19
  • Hosea 11:1-4
—Ask the individuals or groups to answer these questions about their passage(s):
  • In what ways was the Exodus remembered?
  • What does this remembrance of the Exodus say about God?
—As time allows, ask the whole group to list things that might have been different had Israel remained enslaved in Egypt rather than being freed by God.

3. To consider ways to work with God toward deliverance.

☐ A. ACCEPT RESPONSIBILITY
—In advance of the session, prepare to tell Exodus 3:1–4:17 as a story. You might tell the story as a first person narrative from Moses' perspective or from the bush's perspective. Or you might tell it as a third person story.
—After telling the story, summarize the material from "Moses and the Burning Bush," beginning on page 31 of the study book.
—As a group, select a contemporary example of ongoing oppression and discuss: How has God called you, personally, to become involved?
  • How has God called the church to become involved?
  • How have you sought to decline responsibility for the removal of oppression?
  • Can a person remain neutral in the presence of oppression?
  • What one, concrete step might you take to try to reduce the suffering caused by this example of oppression?

☐ B. REFRESH YOUR MEMORY ON THE TEN COMMANDMENTS
—As individuals, and without consulting Bibles or study books, try to list the Ten Commandments from memory. Do not worry about remembering the exact wording or order.
—Compare the lists made from memory with Exodus 20:1-17 or with "The Ten Commandments" on page 34 in the study book.
—Going through the commandments one by one, discuss: To what extent is this commandment relevant to living today?
  • How might abiding by this commandment lessen oppression?
—Ask: What difference does it make if only one individual or one small group of people live by the Ten Commandments if no one else in a community or society does so?

☐ C. READ IT FOR YOURSELF
—Individually or as a group, work through "Read It for Yourself" on page 34 of the study book.
—Share any information you have gained from your preparation or from the "Bible Background" at the end of this lesson in this leader's guide. Recall information about "covenant" from the previous chapter.
—Discuss: What do you think it means to be "a priestly kingdom and a holy nation" within a world where oppression exists?
—Read Exodus 24:1-8. As one person reads the passage aloud a second time, have the rest of the group act out what is happening without words or props.
—Ask: What effect do you think the use of blood had on the people in the covenant ceremony of Exodus 24:1-8? What meanings do you think they might have found?
—Share additional information as appropriate from "Bible Background."

4. To close the session.

☐ A. LET THE BIBLE FORM YOU
—Share information about the situation behind the writing of Psalm 137 from "Let the Bible Form You," found on page 36 of the study book.
—Guide the group through the questions and steps suggested in "Let the Bible Form You." Focus on the deep and raw emotions persons might share with God when contemplating their roles as oppressors and/or victims.

☐ B. NAME THE ENEMIES

—Read Psalm 137 and share information about the psalm from "Let the Bible Form You," page 36 of the study book.

—In two groups study Psalms 92 and 94 to note feelings and images expressed in them concerning "enemies" and "evildoers."

—As a whole group, participate in a responsive prayer. Allow persons to name briefly "enemies" and "evildoers" in their experience. These might be forces in their lives as well as persons or groups. After each naming, the whole group may respond with "Lord, deliver us."

—Pair off to pray for the deliverance of partners from whomever or whatever their "enemy" might be.

☐ C. CLOSE WITH PRAYER

—Offer this prayer or one in your own words: "Faithful God, you do not abandon your people to the power of evil. Grant that those who suffer for the sake of justice may find strength in the cross of Jesus and be filled with your peace now and forever" (from *Daily Prayer: The Worship of God*, prepared by The Office of Worship for the Presbyterian Church [U.S.A.] and the Cumberland Presbyterian Church; Westminster Press, 1987; page 231. Adapted from *Lutheran Book of Worship*, copyright © 1978, by permission of Augsburg Fortress).

BIBLE BACKGROUND

The Book of Exodus tells the story of how God delivered an obscure people from enslavement in Egypt and invited them into a new identity as God's own people. God is the main actor. However, God called the Hebrew fugitive Moses to lead the people on God's behalf.

This session can only deal with a small portion of the entire story. If you can take the time (perhaps an hour or two), you might find it useful to read all forty chapters of Exodus. The story is powerful, and it provides the key to Israel's understanding of its own identity as a people.

If you are interested in more information about the Book of Exodus, one good commentary is *Exodus*, by Terence E. Fretheim, in the Interpretation series (Westminster, 1991).

The Giving and Receiving of the Covenant: Exodus 19:1-9 and Exodus 24:3-8

This "Bible Background" section offers special help if you choose to lead your group through the learning activity 3C related to "Read It for Yourself" on page 34 of the study book.

The Israelites became a people in a special way at Mount Sinai after their escape from Egypt. There, they encountered God who offered them the possibility of relating to God in a way different from the rest of the world.

Exactly two and one-half months after the angel of death passed over their first-born, the Israelites arrived and encamped at Mount Sinai. You might wish to locate Mount Sinai on the map on page 35 in the study book. In Exodus 3:11-12, God had promised Moses that the Israelites would worship God at Mount Horeb (Sinai) as a sign that God had indeed called Moses to lead the people on God's behalf.

At first, in Exodus 19, only Moses deals directly with God. In verses 4-6, God tells Moses three things: what God has unconditionally done for the Israelites, what God asks Israel to do, and what God will do conditionally if Israel does what God asks.

God has rescued Israel from the Egyptians and brought them to deal directly with God. The image of "eagles' wings" is one of nurture and protection: God describes God's self as a mother eagle.

God asks Israel to obey God's voice and to keep God's covenant. Although in Exodus 19–23 God will present Israel with the Ten Commandments and other laws, obeying God's voice demands more than simply following rules and keeping laws. Further, Israel is to obey God's voice not merely because God has commanded something or because something is a good and moral thing independent of God's saying so. Rather Israel should obey God because of the closeness of the relationship between Israel and God.

God has already chosen Israel to be a special people in freeing them from slavery. Israel can now continue to be God's people only by doing as God asks. If Israel will do what God says, then it will be a "treasured possession," a "priestly kingdom," and a "holy nation." These three images describe the same relationship.

Israel is now and can continue to be the people of God. It belongs to God in an especially cherished and loved way. The people will serve as "priests" to the rest of the world, mediating between the other peoples and God. As holy, Israel will be set apart from the ordinary and the usual.

Verses 7-8 say that Moses told God's words to the elders, who were the clan and family heads. The elders then either relayed this message to the people under their care, who then responded, or answered for the people under their care. Either way, the answer was that the people of Israel accepted the condition of obeying God's voice and keeping God's covenant in order to continue as God's own people.

After the actual giving of the covenant in the Ten Commandments and other laws, Exodus 24:3-8 tells of the covenant ceremony through which the Israelites and God formally entered into their agreement. This same ceremony is retold from a different tradition in Exodus 24:1-2, 9-11.

In the version found in verses 3-8, Moses serves as mediator between God and all the people (not just the leaders or the elders). The twelve pillars erected represent all the people in their twelve tribes.

The two types of sacrifices mentioned in verse 5—the burnt offering and the sacrifice of well-being—are described in Leviticus 1 and Leviticus 3. Modern Christians have little idea how important these sacrifices were for the Jews up until the second destruction of the Jerusalem Temple in A.D. 70. We have never worshiped God in this way. For the Israelites, however, the person and the community gave something precious to God in the blood and the smoke of the sacrifice at the altar.

Burnt offerings present a gift from a worshiper's substance. Animals meant food for survival. Giving up a portion of the means of survival demonstrated the worshiper's trust in God to provide what was needed. Moreover, the smoke given off by the burning carcass was thought to be a scent pleasing to God as it rose toward the heavens.

In the offering of well-being, a meal was prepared. This meal was seen as one shared by the worshiper with God and with the community.

The blood that was drained from the animal was viewed as the animal's life-force. As the blood flowed out of the animal, one could observe that life also left the animal. Therefore, blood and life were seen as connected, perhaps even the same. To dash the blood of the sacrifice on the altar was to present the animal's life to God. In verse 8, when the blood is also thrown over all the people, God and the people are joined together in the force of life.

You might want to spend a few moments imagining what it might have been like to participate in a sacrifice or in the covenant ceremony described in Exodus 24. If you are interested, you might also wish to read more about sacrifice in *The Interpreter's Dictionary of the Bible* or other Bible reference books.

CHAPTER 4

GOD
JUDGES
AND
RESTORES
THE
PEOPLE

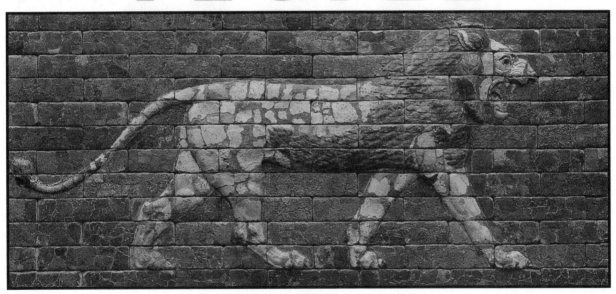

LEARNING MENU

Build your learning menu by selecting one or more learning ideas for each of the Learning Menu headings below:

1. to learn about the prophets	2. to diagnose the problem of human disobedience	3. to ponder alternative ways of living and their consequences	4. to look to God for help	5. to close the session

LEARNING IDEA SELECTIONS

1. To learn about the prophets.

☐ A. CATCH UP TO DATE
—As group members arrive, ask them to read "How Did God's People Get to Babylonia?" on page 39 of the study book and to look especially at the timetable.
—Share and discuss any pieces of new information or surprises.
—Note the dates and events on the timetable when Hosea, Jeremiah, Nehemiah, and Ezra were active. This chapter will cover the period of those four persons' lifetimes—a period of more than 350 years.

☐ B. CREATE YOUR OWN TIME LINE
—Ahead of time, prepare a set of "event cards" using a stack of blank 3 x 5 cards. On each card, write one of the events found on the timetable on page 39 of the study book; but do not include the event's date. Shuffle the completed set of event cards so that they are out of chronological order.
—As group members arrive, invite them to work together to arrange the event cards in chronological order without referring to the study book or other resources. Their time line may be laid out on the floor or on a table top, clipped with clothespins to a string attached to opposite walls, or attached to a wall with masking tape.
—Check the group's time line with the timetable appearing on page 39 of the study book. Discuss any new information or surprises.

☐ C. DEFINE A PROPHET
—Divide the group into smaller groups of three to five members.
—Ask each small group to agree on a definition for the word *prophet* without looking at the study book or other resources.
—Come back together as a whole group and share definitions. Note common and different elements.
—Read or summarize the material found in "What Is a Prophet?" on page 40 of the study book.
—Discuss any points in "What Is a Prophet?" that persons might have found surprising.

☐ D. LOOK FOR TODAY'S PROPHETS
—If you have not already done so, read or summarize the material found in "What Is a Prophet?" on page 40 of the study book.
—Dividing the group into smaller groups, ask the small groups to list the names of persons who fit the description of a prophet in the world today.
—Share lists with the whole group. Discuss: In what ways is each person listed sharing the word God wants shared with the people?
  • For what reasons would you say that today's prophets are or are not like the prophets of the Old Testament?

☐ E. RESEARCH OTHER PROPHETS OF THE BIBLE
—Ahead of time, gather a collection of Bible dictionaries, commentaries on the books of the prophets, and Bibles that include introductions to the books of the Bible.
—Because of the limitations placed by the survey quality of this study, only Hosea and Jeremiah are examined in *Get Acquainted With Your Bible*. This activity provides an opportunity to learn something about other prophets of the Old Testament.

—Assign individuals or teams to find out what they can about the lives, times, and messages of these other prophets:

If you only have a few individuals or teams, ask them to research Isaiah, Ezekiel, Daniel, Amos, and Micah.

If you have a larger number of individuals or teams, ask them to research the prophets mentioned above plus any or all of the following: Joel, Obadiah, Jonah, Nahum, Habakkuk, Zephaniah, Haggai, Zechariah, and Malachi.

—Individuals or teams may use whatever resources they have brought with them, the resources you have provided, and the resources that might be available in your church's library. Research can become time consuming, so you might want to set a suitable time limit.

—Ask individuals or teams to share their research. When all have shared, discuss: What similarities and differences do you find among these prophets?

2. To diagnose the problem of human disobedience.

☐ A. READ THE SIGNS OF THE TIMES
—Read or summarize material from either "The Prophet Hosea and His Times" (page 41 in the study book) or "The Prophet Jeremiah and His Times" (page 42 in the study book). Using the timetable (on page 39) and map (on page 43) from the study book, as well as other information and resources you might have available, help group members see the political, social, moral, and military background for Hosea or Jeremiah at least at a basic level. For example, you might stress that during Hosea's lifetime, Israel was a weak nation both internally and internationally. The section "The Prophet Hosea and His Times" summarizes that situation. Additional information on the situations of Hosea and Jeremiah may be found in "Bible Background" on pages 31–32 in this leader's guide.
—Discuss the ways in which national troubles during the time of Hosea or of Jeremiah might have arisen from human disobedience.
—Ask: What are the "signs of the times" today? In what ways do modern examples of human disobedience lead to local, national, or global problems?

☐ B. HAND DOWN AN INDICTMENT
—Read or summarize the material found in "The Prophet Hosea and His Times" on page 41 of the study book. Call attention to "An Indictment" on page 41 of the study book.
—Invite the group members to imagine themselves as a grand jury. A grand jury's task is to consider whether enough evidence exists to indict a person to be prosecuted in court for a crime. Instruct the group to consider whether enough evidence is available to indict today's American society, and on what charges.
—Add props and your own embellishments to make this activity seem more like an actual grand jury at work. Arrange ahead of time with persons outside your group to come and "testify" before the grand jury as "witnesses." If anyone in your group has ever served on a grand jury, ask her or him to serve as jury foreperson.

☐ C. SYMBOLIZE THE SITUATION
—Sometimes persons express and understand situations better through symbols, pictures, or drama than through words. Jeremiah used several vivid symbols to get his points across.
—Read or summarize the material found in "The Prophet Jeremiah and His Times" on page 42 of the study book.

—On several occasions Jeremiah made his point either by offering a vivid image or by acting out an image so that it became something like a dramatic parable. Assign the following images to individuals or small groups:

- Jeremiah 13:1-11, ruined loincloth
- Jeremiah 18:1-12, potter
- Jeremiah 19:1-13, broken jug
- Jeremiah 24:1-10, two baskets of figs
- Jeremiah 27:1-15, yoke
- Jeremiah 32:1-15, purchase of a field

Each individual or group should look up the related biblical passage in order to summarize the text and image for the whole group.

—Discuss what images, symbols, or drama might be appropriate to express God's message for today.

3. To ponder alternative ways of living and their consequences.

☐ A. EXPLORE THE CHOICES

—If you have not already done so, read or summarize the material in "The Prophet Jeremiah and His Times," found on page 42 of the study book. Also share information from "The Trauma of the Exile," found on page 44 of the study book.

—Divide the group members into small groups of three persons. Ask the small groups to read "Choosing Death Instead of Life" (on page 43 of the study book) and the biblical passages mentioned there. Then ask them to discuss the following questions within their small groups:

- Did the people of Judah "get what they deserved" in the Exile? Why, or why not?
- How might the people of Judah have chosen life?
- In what ways are modern Christians faced with choosing between "life" and "death"?

—After an appropriate length of time, discuss small group responses within the whole group.

☐ B. IGNORE THE PROBLEM

—If you have not already done so, read or summarize the material in "The Prophet Jeremiah and His Times," found on page 42 of the study book.

—Divide the group members into two or more smaller groups. Ask the small groups to read Jeremiah 8:4-12. As they read, they should keep in mind that Jeremiah spoke these words in order to scold the people and their leaders for continuing to act immorally. Note especially verses 10-11, in which Jeremiah condemns the religious leaders for offering easy answers and for saying that everything is all right the way things are.

—Ask the small groups each to write a response to Jeremiah 8:4-12 as if they were the religious leaders opposing Jeremiah.

—Share responses within the whole group. Discuss in what ways people and leaders within today's society and church try to ignore the problems.

4. To look to God for help.

☐ A. LOOK FOR THE HAND OF GOD

—Read or summarize the information in "Return of the Exiles" beginning on page 44 of the study book. Emphasize that the Jews saw their restoration to their homeland as God's doing.

—Discuss in small groups or as a whole group: In what ways do you see the hand of God at work in national or global events?

- What do these events tell you about God?

☐ B. READ IT FOR YOURSELF
—As individuals, small groups, or the whole group, work through "Read It for Yourself" on page 46 of the study book. Be prepared to help the group recall information from previous sessions about the concept of "covenant."
—Discuss: In what ways might this new covenant make a difference for individuals and for humanity as a whole?

5. To close the session.

☐ A. LET THE BIBLE FORM YOU
—Share the background information about Psalm 130 found in "Let the Bible Form You," beginning on page 46 of the study book.
—Lead the group in meditating on Psalm 130. Invite persons to sit comfortably, to close their eyes, and to allow their minds and imaginations to go where they will go as you read Psalm 130 aloud slowly.
—If you wish, guide them through the imagery suggested in the latter half of "Let the Bible Form You."
—Close with the "Psalm Response" or with a prayer.

☐ B. CLOSE WITH PRAYER
—Offer the following prayer or one in your own words: Gracious God: Help us to see your hand at work and to hear your words. Steer us away from easy answers to the world's problems. May we be found doing your will. In Jesus' name. Amen.

BIBLE BACKGROUND

The books of the prophets are not arranged in chronological order. Instead, they are arranged according to their length. Although Jeremiah's book is placed earlier in the Old Testament, Hosea was active around 745 B.C., about 120 years before Jeremiah became a prophet.

In order to appreciate any of the prophets more fully, some knowledge of biblical history, geography, and politics is important. Detailed information is not necessary. However, some basic facts will help. Many of these facts can be discovered by studying the timetable on page 39 of the study book.

For example, one set of basic facts that is crucial to understanding Hosea and Jeremiah is that the Kingdom of Israel over which Saul, David, and Solomon reigned beginning about 1020 B.C. split into two kingdoms after Solomon's death in 928 B.C. The Northern Kingdom was known as Israel and had its capital at Samaria. The Southern Kingdom was known as Judah and had its capital at Jerusalem. Israel was destroyed as an independent nation in 721 B.C. by the Assyrian Empire. Judah was destroyed as an independent nation in 587 B.C. by the Babylonian Empire.

More About Hosea

Hosea, whose name literally means "salvation" or "deliverance," was active as a prophet in the Northern Kingdom of Israel roughly between the years 755 B.C. and 725 B.C. Hosea's Israel was at war with the superpower of Assyria and with itself. His basic message was that although Israel had been unfaithful to God, God's love would never let Israel go.

Hosea's writings are filled with metaphors describing the relationship between God and the people. The major metaphor speaks of God as a loving husband and of the people as an adulterous wife. This metaphor was modeled on Hosea's relationship with his unfaithful wife Gomer as described in the first three chapters of his book. Throughout the book, accusations and announcements of punishment are outweighed by words of love, comfort, and healing.

Hosea's time had more low lights than highlights:

—After King Jeroboam [jer-uh-BOH-uhm] II's forty-year reign of stability and prosperity, King Zechariah [zak-uh-RI-uh] (no relation to the prophet by that name) ruled for only six months before he was assassinated by Shallum [SHAL-uhm].

—King Shallum ruled for only one month before he was assassinated by Menahem [MEN-uh-hem].

—King Menahem ruled for seven years, but during that time he was forced to pay tribute (extortion or "protection" money) to the Assyrian Empire.

—After Menahem's death, King Pekahiah [pek-uh-HI-uh] ruled two years before he was assassinated by Pekah [PEE-kuh].

—King Pekah ruled five years, during which Israel joined Syria in a revolt against Assyria. Israel and Syria attacked Judah when the latter refused to join their alliance. Assyria came to Judah's defense, defeated Israel, and deported part of its population in 733 B.C. One year later, King Pekah was assassinated by Hoshea [hoh-SHEE-uh].

—King Hoshea first submitted to and then rebelled against Assyria. Within eleven years, in 721 B.C., Assyria destroyed Israel as a nation.

Do not worry about remembering all these names and dates. Do not expect your group members to remember them either. However, you should keep in mind the political chaos suffered by Israel during Hosea's lifetime. During these crises, Hosea accused his people of trusting military strength, alliances with superpowers, and false idols more than God. But he also spoke strong words of hope.

More About Jeremiah

Just as Hosea came forward to speak on God's behalf during a time of spiritual and political crisis in Israel, so Jeremiah did the same a century later in Judah. After Israel's fall, Judah retained its national identity. The power of the Assyrian Empire diminished; but a new superpower, Babylonia, arose in the region that today is called Iraq.

Many of Jeremiah's prophecies were probably collected and written down by his secretary, Baruch [BAIR-uhk]. However, the book itself does not appear to be arranged in chronological order. If you want to read the entire Book of Jeremiah, you might want to find a good commentary or other guide to follow.

Two features of the Book of Jeremiah are especially worth noting. First, there are the details of the opposition presented to Jeremiah's prophecies. One should expect Jeremiah to be unpopular in that he consistently urged Judah to surrender to Babylonia rather than resist. On at least one occasion, Jeremiah was arrested for treason (Jeremiah 37:11-21); at least once, an attempt was made on his life (Jeremiah 38:1-13).

Second, the Book of Jeremiah is filled with his laments—expressions of his spiritual struggles with God. Jeremiah fought aloud with God over preaching the unpopular message God insisted must be conveyed.

The national events of Jeremiah's lifetime were troubled:

—Jeremiah began to prophesy during the long and progressive reign of King Josiah [joh-SI-uh], who ruled from 640 B.C. until 609 B.C. During this time, Assyria's control over the region began to weaken. Judah began to assert its national independence. In 621 B.C., King Josiah initiated a religious reform. But in 609 B.C., King Josiah was killed in battle when the Egyptian army marched through Judah on its way to assist the Assyrians in their war against the Babylonians.

—By 605 B.C., Babylonia began to assert its influence over Judah and to demand tribute. In 602 B.C., King Jehoiakim [ji-HOI-uh-kim] revolted against Babylonia. After a long siege, during which Jehoiakim died, Babylonia captured Jerusalem. The Babylonians removed King Jehoiachin [ji-HOI-uh-kin], Jehoiakim's son, from the throne and imprisoned him in Babylonia.

—Zedekiah [zed-uh-KI-uh] was made king of Judah by the Babylonians but later rebelled. After another war and long siege, in 587 B.C., the Babylonians again captured Jerusalem. King Zedekiah was forced to watch his sons executed, to be blinded, and then to be imprisoned in Babylonia. The palace and the Temple were looted and destroyed. Judah's wealthy and skilled people were deported to Babylonia.

—Gedaliah [ged-uh-LI-uh] was named governor over Judah by the Babylonians. Because of Jeremiah's pro-Babylonian views, he was permitted to remain in what was left of Jerusalem. However, in 583 B.C., Gedaliah was assassinated. Many Judean officials fled to Egypt taking Jeremiah with them. Jeremiah apparently died there.

CHAPTER 5

GOD
COMES
TO
THE
PEOPLE

LEARNING MENU

Build your learning menu by selecting one or more
learning ideas for each of the Learning Menu headings
below:

1. to look at
what the Bible
claims about
Jesus

2. to consider
what Jesus
shows us about
God

3. to explore what
group members
believe about
Jesus

4. to close the
session

LEARNING IDEA SELECTIONS

1. To look at what the Bible claims about Jesus.

☐ A. TALK ABOUT NAMES

—For this activity you will need one or more Bible dictionaries, one or more books telling the meaning of names (these may be found at public libraries or in the homes of expectant parents), and 3 x 5 cards.

—As group members arrive, hand them each a 3 x 5 card; and ask them to list in a column on the left side their name and names of members of their family. If they have children, ask them to recall how they came to give the names they did to their children. Also, all members should recall any stories around how they came to be given their own name. They might wish to make brief notes about these stories on the right side of their card.

—Then ask the group members to look up the names on their card in the name books. If the name is from the Bible, they should also look it up in a Bible dictionary to see what meanings and Bible stories are associated with that name. They should note on the back of their card the meanings given for the names.

—Then ask each group member to share briefly a meaning or a story about a name within his or her family.

—Tell the group members that often in the Bible, persons were given names with special meanings attached. They might remember from Chapter 1 that the names *Adam* and *Eve* had special meanings. So did the name *Jesus*.

—Read Matthew 1:18-23.

—Ask the group members to look up *Jesus* and *Emmanuel* in a Bible dictionary and to share any information and insights.

—Compare these learnings with the claims revealed by the other names for Jesus listed in "What's in a Name?" on page 50 of the study book.

☐ B. DISCOVER THE MESSIAH

—Plan to have Bibles and Bible commentaries for group members to use.

—The earliest and most important claim the church made about Jesus was that he is the Messiah. Summarize the information found in "Who Is Jesus?" beginning on page 51 of the study book, or give group members time to read that section. Ask whether this information is different from ideas members already have about the meaning of *Messiah* and *Christ*.

—As individuals, pairs, or small groups (depending on the size of your group), have members look up one or more of these passages to see what expectations about the Messiah Jews found in the Old Testament:
  • 2 Samuel 7:12-17
  • Isaiah 9:1-7
  • Isaiah 11:1-12
  • Isaiah 52:13–53:12
  • Jeremiah 23:5-6
  • Micah 5:2-4
  • Zechariah 9:9-11

—If time permits, ask group members also to look up these passages in commentaries. Take time to share what was learned about each passage.

—The diversity in expectations stems from the fact that different persons wrote different passages at different times and places to meet different circumstances. However, in the first century, Christians read these and other passages after having met Jesus and having witnessed his resurrection appearances. They reinterpreted the Jewish expectations about a Messiah to explain what they saw in Jesus.

2. To consider what Jesus shows us about God.

☐ A. LEARN ABOUT GOD FROM JESUS
—Summarize the information found in "What Did Jesus Do?" on page 50 of the study book, or provide time for group members to read that section.
—Divide the group members into four small groups. Assign one of the following areas and related list of stories to each group:

Stories about Jesus teaching
- Matthew 5–7
- Luke 15–16

Stories about Jesus healing
- Matthew 8:1-17
- Luke 8:26-56

Stories about Jesus' crucifixion
- Mark 15
- Luke 23

Stories about Jesus' resurrection
- Matthew 28
- John 20–21

—Ask each small group to assume that all they know about Jesus relates to their group's area. For example, if they are assigned "Stories about Jesus teaching," they know nothing about his healing ministry, his death, or his resurrection. They are to read the stories listed and any other stories related to their category that they wish. Without drawing from any other information, they are to answer these two questions:
 1. If all you had were the stories related to your area, what would you learn about Jesus?
 2. If this was all you knew about Jesus, what would it teach you about God?
—After an appropriate length of time, have each small group report to the total group.

☐ B. PICTURE WHAT SALVATION LOOKS LIKE
—Provide group members with scissors and with magazines containing lots of pictures.
—One of the basic claims of the New Testament is that God sent Jesus in order to offer humanity salvation. To start a discussion of what salvation is, ask group members to browse through the magazines you have supplied and to cut out up to three pictures each that help them describe salvation.
—Ask group members to share their pictures.
—Work together as a group to come up with a definition of salvation.
—One of the questions you might ask to encourage conversation is, What does Jesus save us from and for?

3. To explore what group members believe about Jesus.

☐ A. LIST LIFE BELIEFS
—You will need some scrap paper to write on and pencils for everyone.
—A belief may be described as something persons arrange their lives around or stake their lives on. The statement about "Belief" in the study book, page 53, says that the word *belief* refers to desiring something, loving something, or trusting something.

—Ask group members to make a list of their life beliefs. Another way to give them this assignment is to ask, What is it that drives the way you live?
—Permit those who wish to do so to share briefly their life beliefs.

☐ B. LOOK FOR PROOF
—Prior to the session, you will need to recruit three to five persons who meet these criteria: a deep, mature faith; a willingness and ability to talk about their faith in Christ without becoming defensive; and a willingness to meet with your group members. Your pastor might be able to suggest some individuals.
—Summarize the information in "Looking for Proof" on page 53 of the study book.
—Introduce to your group members the persons you have invited to share about their faith. These are persons who have decided they have found sufficient proof to believe that Jesus is in fact the Christ.
—Lead a discussion around such questions as: How did you come to believe that Jesus is the Christ?
  • What does it mean for you to say that Jesus is the Christ?
  • What sorts of proof did you look for? What dead ends did you find in your search for proof?
  • What role did the Bible play in helping you arrive at belief? What role did the church play?
  • What doubts have you had? How have you dealt with those doubts?
  • What does it feel like to believe that Jesus is the Christ?
  • How would you help someone else arrive at belief?
—Be sure to provide an opportunity for all group members to join in the discussion.

☐ C. READ IT FOR YOURSELF
—Provide Bibles, Bible dictionaries, concordances, commentaries, and pencils for this activity.
—Work through individually or as a group "Read It for Yourself" on page 55 of the study book.
—Share any information you have gained from your own preparation or from the "Bible Background" at the end of this lesson in this leader's guide. Also draw attention to the material found in "Who Is Jesus?" and "Looking for Proof" on pages 51–53 of the study book.
—Discuss the questions listed at the end of "Read It for Yourself." See the "Bible Background" for ideas for the directions this discussion might take.

☐ D. THINK ABOUT HOW TO HAVE FAITH
—The study book contains a viewpoint on faith that says, "Faith does not come by exertion of the will but by its surrender."
—Ask group members to discuss this viewpoint. How do they understand it? Do they agree with it? Why, or why not? Can they offer anecdotes that show whether it is an accurate statement?
—Ask a group member to read "One Man's Struggle to Believe," page 54 in the study book, aloud. Then form small groups to discuss the question: How does John Wesley's struggle with faith prove or disprove this viewpoint?

☐ E. PLAN HOW TO TEACH FAITH
—Ask the group members to discuss the following questions:
  • What do you want your children (or your nieces and nephews or grandchildren or the children of friends) to know about Jesus?
  • How would you go about teaching them?

4. To close the session.

A. LET THE BIBLE FORM YOU
—Share the information about Psalm 24 found in "Let the Bible Form You" on page 56 of the study book.
—Guide the group members through the steps found at the end of the section.

B. PRAY TOGETHER
—Close by joining together in saying the prayer printed on page 57 of the study book.

BIBLE BACKGROUND

Matthew 16:13-28

This story about Peter's confession that Jesus is the Messiah is also told in Mark 8:27–9:1 and Luke 9:18-27. You might want to read those accounts to see in what ways they differ. However, in this lesson you will be looking at Matthew's version.

In this story one of Jesus' disciples realizes and states for the first time that Jesus is the Messiah. This is the basic belief claim of Christianity. However, in the exchange that follows, Jesus makes sure Peter and the other disciples see that his messiahship leads to suffering rather than to earthly glory.

The setting is the region around Caesarea Philippi, to the north and east of Galilee. Jesus and the disciples were probably in the area known today as the Golan Heights. We do not know for sure, but perhaps it is significant that Jesus went off to a region physically removed from Galilee and Jerusalem in order to reflect on his identity and his mission as God's Messiah.

Jesus refers to himself as "Son of Man" in verse 13. Scholars are not entirely sure what this title meant in Jesus' time. However, the Gospels tell of Jesus using it many times to refer to himself. Christians have understood it as another way to speak of Jesus as the Messiah.

People often mistook Jesus for one of the prophets because of the manner of his teaching. Also, there were traditions looking for Elijah or Jeremiah to return to earth in the last days in order to prepare the Jews for the coming of the Messiah.

After Peter confessed Jesus as the Messiah, Jesus noted that no human being taught Peter this insight. Peter's awareness was a gift of God's grace

In verse 18, there is a play on the words in the original Greek language between Peter's name *Petros* and the word for rock, *petra*. In Aramaic, the language Jesus and his disciples spoke, Peter's name and the word for rock were identical, *kepha*. Jesus might also have chosen to call his friend "Peter," or "Rock," in order to challenge him away from the kind of wavering Peter displayed on the night of Jesus' arrest (Matthew 26:69-75).

Only in verse 18 here and in Matthew 18:17 does the word *church* appear in the Gospels. The reference to the "gates of Hades" means that not even the power of death can overwhelm the church built upon the confession that Jesus is the Messiah.

The "keys of the kingdom" in verse 19 refer to the keys that a king would have entrusted to the chief steward of the royal household. They were symbols of trust and authority.

In verses 21-23, Jesus teaches the disciples about his coming suffering and death. Peter's rebuke of Jesus shows that Peter only understood part of the truth about the Messiah. While God had given Peter the insight to see that Jesus was the Messiah, Peter still had the same expectations for what the Messiah would be like that other Jews of his time had.

Verse 23 sounds a lot like Matthew 4:10, when Jesus tells Satan to stop tempting him. Note how Peter moved from being a rock in verse 18 to being a stumbling block in verse 23.

Jesus plainly understood his identity and mission, and that of his followers, to be one of self-denial, suffering, and servanthood.

CHAPTER 6

GOD
CALLS
A NEW
PEOPLE

LEARNING MENU

Build your learning menu by selecting one or more learning ideas for each of the Learning Menu headings below:

1. to look at the beginning of the church at the first Christian Pentecost

2. to consider what the presence and gifts of the Holy Spirit mean for Christians

3. to explore conversion and the Christian life

4. to consider group members' place within the church

5. to close the session

LEARNING IDEA SELECTIONS

1. To look at the beginning of the church at the first Christian Pentecost.

☐ A. EXPERIENCE PENTECOST

—This learning activity can serve as a good introduction to Pentecost as the experience that launched the Christian church and as one of the high festival days of the church year.

—In the days before this session, make the following preparations: Enlist one or more helpers to assist you with the various "special effects" you will use in this activity.

Decorate your classroom festively with Pentecost symbols and colors. Red crepe paper and bunting might be draped around the room. The red paraments used in the sanctuary on Pentecost might be borrowed and prominently displayed. Red balloons might be filled with helium and attached to tables and chairs. Be creative!

Obtain several room fans and strobe lights for use in special effects when appropriate portions of the Pentecost story are read (Acts 2:1-4).

Record a dramatic reading or retelling of the Pentecost story, based on Acts 2.

—As group members arrive, welcome them and invite them to sit and wait "here in Jerusalem as the Master told us to do."

—Play the recording of the Pentecost story. Use the fans and strobe lights at the appropriate points.

—After the recording has concluded, ask: What is Pentecost all about?

—Summarize the material from "Jewish Pentecost and Christian Pentecost" on page 59 of the study book.

☐ B. CONSIDER HOW TO CELEBRATE PENTECOST

—Read Acts 2, or tell the story of Pentecost in your own words. Summarize the material from "The Acts of the Apostles" (page 59 in the study book), "Jewish Pentecost and Christian Pentecost" (page 59 in the study book), and "Filled With the Holy Spirit" (page 60 in the study book).

—Talk as a group about how Pentecost is celebrated in your local church. Discuss whether Pentecost is considered a major day in the church year. If your church does not have a big celebration on Pentecost, discuss how you think Pentecost might be celebrated within a worship service.

☐ C. HEAR ABOUT JEWISH PENTECOST

—Pentecost originally was and still is a Jewish festival day. Invite a local rabbi or other Jewish leader to share about the origin, meaning, and modern celebration of Pentecost within Judaism.

—**Or,** ask a group member in advance to prepare a report on the origins of the Jewish celebration of Pentecost as found in Leviticus 23:15-21.

☐ D. REFLECT ON RELIGIOUS FEELINGS

—One way to think about Christian Pentecost is to consider it more as an experience than as an event. There can be no doubt that whatever else happened on that Day of Pentecost told about in Acts 2, the disciples gathered in Jerusalem experienced God in a deeply moving way.

—Distribute paper and pencils to the group members. Ask them to reflect on the following questions and to write their responses:
- What was your "most religious" moment?
- What did you experience then?
- How did you feel at that time?

• How did you express your feelings at that "most religious" moment?
—Offer an opportunity for any persons who wish to share about their reflections to do so.
—Read aloud Acts 2:5-13.
—If you have not already done so, summarize the information found in "Jewish Pentecost and Christian Pentecost" on page 59 of the study book and "Filled With the Holy Spirit" on page 60 of the study book.
—Discuss: What do you think the disciples did that caused some people to think that they were "filled with new wine"—that is, drunk?
• Has there ever been a moment when you were so filled with religious feelings that someone might have mistaken you for being drunk? What happened?

2. To consider what the presence and gifts of the Holy Spirit mean for Christians.

☐ A. FIND A WAY TO EXPRESS HOW YOU EXPERIENCE GOD'S PRESENCE
—Read aloud Acts 2:1-4. Note how this passage uses metaphor or symbols to talk about what the presence of the Holy Spirit was like. Luke does not say that the Holy Spirit appeared as wind or fire. Instead, he describes the Holy Spirit as being "like the rush of a violent wind" and as coming upon the disciples in "divided tongues, as of fire." Add information from "Filled With the Holy Spirit" on page 60 of the study book.
—Have available paper, pencils, colored markers, modeling clay, and a few other craft materials. Ask persons to reflect on how they might express their own experience of the presence of God in their lives. Then invite them to create something from the materials available that expresses what the presence of God is like for them.
—Offer time for persons to share their expression of God's presence.

☐ B. STUDY MORE ABOUT THE HOLY SPIRIT
—Divide the group members into five small groups.
—Assign one of the passages mentioned in "What's in a Name?" on page 60 of the study book to each small group.
—Ask the small groups to study their passage and to prepare to share what they learn about the Holy Spirit from that passage.
—After each small group has reported, work as a whole group to describe what can be said about the Holy Spirit based on these Bible passages.

☐ C. LOOK AT WHAT THE HOLY SPIRIT GIVES
—Ask persons to read aloud 1 Corinthians 12:1-11 (about some of the gifts of the Holy Spirit) and Galatians 5:22-26 (about some of the fruits of the Holy Spirit). Discuss how these gifts and fruits benefit the individual Christian as well as the whole church.
—Distribute different colored sheets of construction paper to the members of the group. Ask each person to write his or her name at the top of the sheet and then to place the sheet in the middle of the table or the floor.
—Ask each person to write on the sheets belonging to the other members of the group what gift or fruit of the Holy Spirit they see in that person. The gifts or fruits that they name do not have to be the same ones listed in the passages from 1 Corinthians 12 or Galatians 5.
—When everyone has written something on everyone else's sheet, let each person claim and look at his or her sheet.
—Discuss: How did it feel to think about what the Holy Spirit had given to another person?

• How did it feel to see what someone else believes you have received as a gift or fruit of the Holy Spirit?

3. To explore conversion and the Christian life.

☐ A. MAKE YOUR POINTS ABOUT JESUS
—Divide the group members into small groups of three persons.
—Assign each small group this task: If you had to say exactly six things about Jesus to someone who had never heard of him, what would those six things be? Everyone in the group must agree to the list of six things.
—Write on newsprint or chalkboard the lists each small group reports.
—Then work as a whole group to come up with only one list of six things the group would want to say about Jesus.
—Compare the group's list with the main points of Peter's sermon as summarized in "The First Christian Sermon" on page 61 of the study book. Note that Peter's sermon may have expressed the best six points for his time and place but that if your group came up with a different six points, your points might in fact be more appropriate for telling about Jesus to the people around you.

☐ B. SHARE THE DIFFERENCE CHRIST MAKES IN YOUR LIFE
—Read or share the information in the introductory paragraphs in "Changes From Enemies Into Followers" on page 62 of the study book.
—Divide the group members into three small groups. Assign Peter, Saul, or Cornelius to each group.
—Ask each small group to report on the conversion of their person based on the information contained in "Changes From Enemies Into Followers" and the Bible passage mentioned with each person.
—After each small group has reported, pair off the members of the group. The members of each pair are to take turns telling about a time of conversion they might have experienced in their life. However, note with the group that not everyone has one, dramatic conversion experience. For some persons, conversion occurs gradually or beyond the edges of their awareness. A way that these persons might find helpful to talk about their conversion is to answer the question: How am I different today than I might have been without Christ in my life?

☐ C. READ IT FOR YOURSELF
—Individually, in small groups, or in the whole group, work through "Read It for Yourself" on page 63 of the study book. Be prepared to add appropriate information from your own preparation or from the "Bible Background" in this chapter of this leader's guide.
—An additional activity related to this one would be to have the group or small groups write Paul's resume as if he were applying for a job as a missionary. More information about Paul may be found in 2 Corinthians 11:16-33; Galatians 1:11-24; and Philippians 3:4b-14.

☐ D. COMPARE THE MARKS OF YOUR CHURCH
—In groups of three, determine the three top stories about what is taking place in your local church that are circulating at the moment.
—List these stories on newsprint or chalkboard as the groups report.
—Read Acts 2:43-47, and draw attention to "Marks of the Church" on page 62 of the study book.
—Discuss: How do the top stories about what is going on in our church compare with the marks of the church found in Acts 2:43-47?

4. To consider group members' place within the church.

☐ A. UNDERSTAND WHAT YOU NEED TO DO TO BE A CHRISTIAN
—The section "What Do I Need to Do to Be a Christian?" on page 63 of the study book lists the basic steps for becoming a Christian. You may adapt this list as necessary or make available copies of the vows of membership used by your congregation.
—Remind the group members that according to Acts 2:37, those who heard Peter's sermon at the first Christian Pentecost were so moved by his words about Jesus that they asked, "What should we do?"
—Have your group members read "What Do I Need to Do to Be a Christian?" or have them read copies of the membership or baptismal vows used by your congregation.
—Ask: Is there anything else you can think of that you need to do in order to be a Christian? If so, what would that be?
—Without pressuring, encourage anyone who has not yet committed himself or herself to Christ or joined the congregation to speak with your pastor.

☐ B. LOOK BEYOND YOURSELVES
—Be sure to have sheets of paper and pencils.
—Read Acts 1:6-8. Draw the group members' attention to the map "The Outward Spread of Christianity" on page 61 of the study book.
—Explain that the map shows the way in which Christianity spread outward in widening circles from the first disciples gathered in Jerusalem.
—Invite the group members individually or in small groups to draw another map with your community in the center. Ask them to indicate how far Christianity spreads outward from your church.
—Have persons or small groups share their maps with the total group.
—Discuss: How might we be involved with helping Christianity to spread outward from here?

5. To close the session.

☐ A. LET THE BIBLE FORM YOU
—Share the information about Acts 2 and Joel 2:28-32 found in the first half of "Let the Bible Form You" on page 64 of the study book.
—Guide the group through the meditation on Joel 2:28-32 found in the second half of "Let the Bible Form You," following the words *Try this.*

☐ B. CLOSE WITH PRAYER
—Offer this prayer or one in your own words:
"O God, the Holy Spirit,
   come to us, and among us;
   come as the wind, and cleanse us;
   come as the fire, and burn;
   come as the dew, and refresh;
convict, convert, and consecrate
   many hearts and lives
    to our great good
    and to thy greater glory;
and this we ask for Jesus Christ's sake. Amen."
(From *An Invitation to the Holy Spirit,* by Eric Milner-White; The Society for Promoting Christian Knowledge.)

BIBLE BACKGROUND

Acts 16

For the general background to the Book of the Acts of the Apostles, you might wish to refresh your memory by reading "The Acts of the Apostles" on page 59 of the study book.

Much of the Book of Acts is taken up by accounts of three missionary journeys by the apostle Paul throughout the northern Mediterranean world. Chapter 16 presents several episodes during the second missionary journey as Paul, Silas, and Timothy travel through Asia Minor (now known as Turkey) and Macedonia (now the northern part of Greece). This journey of over 2,000 miles is covered in only a few chapters, so one might well imagine the many other adventures and the less eventful hard walking and hard work encountered by these early Christian missionaries.

As you read through Acts 16 for yourself, you might want to keep in mind the theme of the news about Jesus Christ being shared across cultural barriers. Christianity began within Judaism. But many of those to whom Paul preached were Greek-speaking Gentiles (non-Jews). Paul and his companions had to find ways to translate the gospel from one culture into another.

In the learning activity based on "Read It for Yourself," you will give attention to four of the main characters appearing in Acts 16. The following will provide insights into the activities and characters of those persons based on the material found in that chapter.

Paul:

—Paul appears to be the leader on this missionary trip. For autobiographical material about him, see the references listed in the optional part of the activity "Read It for Yourself" on page 41 of this leader's guide.

—Verses 6-10 portray Paul as someone seeking to be sensitive to what God's Spirit might instruct him to do.

—In verses 16-24, Paul and Silas are arrested, beaten, and jailed for healing a mentally ill slave girl. Her illness had been a source of income for her owners. It is curious that according to verse 18, Paul's apparent motive for healing the girl was that she finally got on his nerves after several days of following them around and loudly proclaiming who they were.

—In verses 25-34, Paul and Silas refuse to run from jail when an earthquake opens the doors and their chains. Instead, they seize the opportunity to witness to their jailer.

Timothy

—Timothy was the son of a Jewish-Christian woman and a Greek (Gentile) father. In the eyes of the Jews, Timothy was thereby also a Jew. In order not to offend any Jews they might meet on their trip, he consented to Paul's insistence that he be circumcised, which would have involved a painful ritual. This fact implies Timothy's willingness to undergo personal hardship for the sake of spreading the gospel. He also embodied a bridge between the Jewish and Gentile cultures.

Lydia:

—Lydia only appears in this chapter. She is described as a wealthy merchant, probably a Gentile converted to Judaism, then living in the important Macedonian city of Philippi. Lydia found herself receptive to Paul's preaching and was baptized into the Christian faith, along with her entire household.

—By inviting Paul and Silas into her home, she became a good example of the Christian virtue of hospitality.

—It is probable that the Philippian Christians continued to meet in Lydia's house. By the fact that she is named in Acts, we might assume that in spite of being a woman in a male-oriented culture, she became an important leader of the Christian church.

the jailer:

—We do not even know the jailer's name. From verses 23-24, we might guess that he was something of a nameless bureaucrat who just followed his orders. Verse 27 implies that he so identified with his job that he was prepared to commit suicide when he thought the prisoners had escaped after the earthquake.

—The fact that Paul and Silas had not tried to escape when they could so struck the jailer that he was immediately converted to Christianity and was instructed in the faith the rest of that night. Like Lydia, he and his entire household were baptized. Also like Lydia, the jailer offered hospitality as he washed the wounds of Paul and Silas and fed them.

CHAPTER 7

GOD
CALLS US
TO LIVE
IN HOPE

LEARNING MENU

Build your learning menu by selecting one or more
learning ideas for each of the Learning Menu headings
below:

1. to think about
what faith might
mean when group
members are
faced with trouble

2. to explore some
of the kinds of
encouragement
the Bible offers
Christians in
trouble

3. to look for
avenues of hope
and faith in the
lives of group
members

4. to close the
session (and the
unit)

LEARNING IDEA SELECTIONS

1. To think about what faith might mean when group members are faced with trouble.

☐ A. EXAMINE YOUR MOTIVES
—As group members arrive ask them to work individually on "A Christian Balance Sheet" on page 67 of the study book.
—Divide the group members into small groups of three. Ask each group to reflect on their work on "A Christian Balance Sheet" and to answer the question, In what ways is it a good deal, or a not so good deal, to be a Christian?
—Share the small group responses.
—Discuss: Why are you a Christian?
  • To what extent are you a Christian because of what you expect to get out of it?
  • What kind of things might discourage you from or persuade you against remaining a Christian?
  • What would you never give up in order to remain a Christian?
  • Would you be willing to give up all your property for the sake of being a Christian?
  • Would you be willing to die for the sake of being a Christian?

☐ B. LOOK FOR TROUBLE
—As group members arrive invite them to list on a common sheet of newsprint their responses to this question: What kinds of trouble might American Christians face in their lives today?
—When a lengthy list has been written and it is time for the session to begin, underline those troubles that members of the group say they or immediate family members who are Christians have faced during the past year.
—Place plus signs (or crosses) in front of those troubles that members say Christians might face specifically and only because they are Christians.
—Discuss: Which troubles are only part of the human situation, and which troubles are the crosses Christians sometimes bear simply because they are Christians?

☐ C. HEAR ABOUT PERSECUTION
—Well in advance of the session, invite a speaker who has witnessed or suffered the persecution of Christians in some part of the world. Your pastor might be able to help you locate such a speaker. Let the speaker know the amount of time available to speak and the context of your group's interest in hearing about the modern persecution of Christians. Be sure to ask him or her to speak about the spiritual resources available to Christians suffering persecution.

2. To explore some of the kinds of encouragement the Bible offers Christians in trouble.

☐ A. ADD TO A LIST OF FAITHFUL PEOPLE
—Divide the group members into a number of small groups. Assign each group one or more of the persons listed in "What's in a Name?" on page 68 of the study book. Ask the groups to report on why their persons were included in the list and what about their persons' examples might be helpful to Christians facing troubles. Groups may draw upon previous study, the material included in "What's in a Name?" and the biblical references.

—Because all but one of the examples from Hebrews 11 are men, tell the groups that each group may nominate one biblical, historical, or contemporary woman for inclusion in the list of the faithful. Allow time for groups to discuss their nominations.

—Share nominations and reasons. Discuss ways in which these additional examples of faith might help Christians in trouble.

☐ B. CREATE A PICTURE POEM
—Divide the group members into two groups.
—Share the concept of a picture poem: A picture poem places words into the shape of an image, object, or symbol that bears some relation or relevance to the words.

Jonah did not want to do as God asked him to. He ran away to sea. But God used a storm to make him listen and act.

—Assign one of the following Bible verses to each group:

"Blessed is anyone who endures temptation. Such a one has stood the test and will receive the crown of life that the Lord has promised to those who love him" (James 1:12).

"Endure trials for the sake of discipline. God is treating you as children; for what child is there whom a parent does not discipline?" (Hebrews 12:7).

—Instruct each small group to design a picture using their Bible verse.
—Share the results, and discuss any insights persons might have gained into the verse from working on or viewing the picture poem.
—If you have access to a calligrapher, copies of calligraphied versions of these picture poems might make treasured gifts to give to group members as "graduation presents" for completing their study of Get Acquainted With Your Bible.

☐ C. EXPLORE THE BOOK OF REVELATION
—Using lecture and discussion, guide the group through the material presented in "The Last Book" (beginning on page 67 in the study book) and "Glimpses of Eternity" (beginning on page 69 in the study book).
—One way of getting into this material is to summarize the information from "The Last Book" and then to ask group members to read Revelation 21:1–22:6. As they read, ask them to write notes about all the imagery and other aspects of the passage that they do not understand or wish to learn more about. Provide time for them to research those puzzling portions using "Glimpses of Eternity" and any Bible reference books you have on hand. You might ask members to use footnotes, commentaries, and other resources to explore the Old Testament passages to which many of the images and ideas of this passage refer.

—Another way to get into the material is to read aloud Revelation 21:1–22:6 and then to ask group members to express through drawing, clay, poetry, or another creative medium some image that stuck in their minds. Be sure to allow time for sharing and discussion.

☐ D. LOOK THROUGH DIFFERENT LENSES
—If you have not already done so, summarize the material found in "The Last Book" (beginning on page 67 in the study book) and "Glimpses of Eternity" (beginning on page 69 in the study book).
—The last paragraph in "Glimpses of Eternity" describes the Book of Revelation "as offering a set of lenses through which to view reality, instead of always seeing reality through the lenses the world insists upon."
—Allow time for group members to browse through newspapers and news magazines you have collected over the past week or two. Ask: What news stories look different to you if you view them through specifically Christian lenses rather than through worldly lenses?
  • Or, What looks different to you in this news story because you are a Christian?

☐ E. DISCUSS HEAVEN
—If you have not already done so, summarize the material found in "The Last Book" (beginning on page 67 in the study book) and "Glimpses of Eternity" (beginning on page 69 in the study book).
—Draw the group members' attention to "You Won't Find *That* in Heaven" on page 71 in the study book.
—Discuss: How do these descriptions from Revelation 21–22 fit your previous understandings about heaven or being eternally in the presence of God?
  • What other things do you hope might be absent from heaven?
  • How do you think this idea of heaven might help or not help persons who are suffering trouble or persecution?

3. To look for avenues of hope and faith in the lives of group members.

☐ A. IMAGINE YOUR CHRISTIAN COMMITMENT
—Draw the group members' attention to "Images of Christian Commitment" on page 67 of the study book.
—Read 2 Timothy 2:1-13.
—Divide the group members into small groups of three. Ask each small group to list three additional images that depict what a completely committed Christian might look like.
—Take time to share the images.
—If someone in the group is talented at drawing and the images lend themselves, ask that person to draw those images on newsprint.

☐ B. READ IT FOR YOURSELF
—Individually, in small groups, or as a whole group, work through "Read It for Yourself" on page 71 of the study book.
—Allow the first part of the material in "Read It for Yourself" to serve as a time to remember past chapters in *Get Acquainted With Your Bible*. Share the information from "Bible Background" in this chapter of this leader's guide and material from *Get Acquainted With Your Bible* only after group members have exhausted what they recall.

☐ C. AFFIRM YOUR FAITH
—The entire Bible is a resource through which God helps us to live in faith

and in hope. *Get Acquainted With Your Bible* has sought to help you and your group members to discover faith and hope in some of the most significant portions of the Bible.

—Divide the group members into small groups. Ask each group to develop its own affirmation of faith based on the Bible passages covered in each chapter of *Get Acquainted With Your Bible*. The one rule in developing these affirmations of faith is that groups may not use the chapter titles in their affirmations of faith.

—Groups might state one affirmation for each chapter. Or, they might write an affirmation based on their learnings taken as a whole. They might write their affirmation in prose or poetry or song. Let them be creative.

—Allow time for groups to share their affirmations of faith with one another. If time allows, print the affirmations of faith on newsprint and have the whole group say each one aloud as an act of worship. Using one, several, or all the affirmations of faith might be one way to close the session.

4. To close the session (and the unit).

☐ A. LET THE BIBLE FORM YOU

—Share the information about Psalm 103 found in the first part of "Let the Bible Form You" on page 72 of the study book.

—Lead the group members in one or more of the three experiments for letting Psalm 103 form you as found in the latter part of "Let the Bible Form You."

—Encourage group members to continue their study of the Bible through personal study and through other group studies in your church.

☐ B. CLOSE WITH AFFIRMATIONS

—If you had the group members develop affirmations of faith as suggested above, use these affirmations in some way for closing worship.

—Encourage group members to continue their study of the Bible through personal study and through other group studies in your church.

☐ C. CLOSE WITH PRAYER

—Close with the prayer printed on the inside back cover of the study book or with a prayer in your own words.

—Encourage group members to continue their study of the Bible through personal study and through other group studies in your church.